K Imagine Pub ©

All rights reserved

No part of this publication may be reproduced, distributed, or transmitted in any form or by any means, including photocopying, recording, without the prior written permission of the publisher

This Book Belongs to :

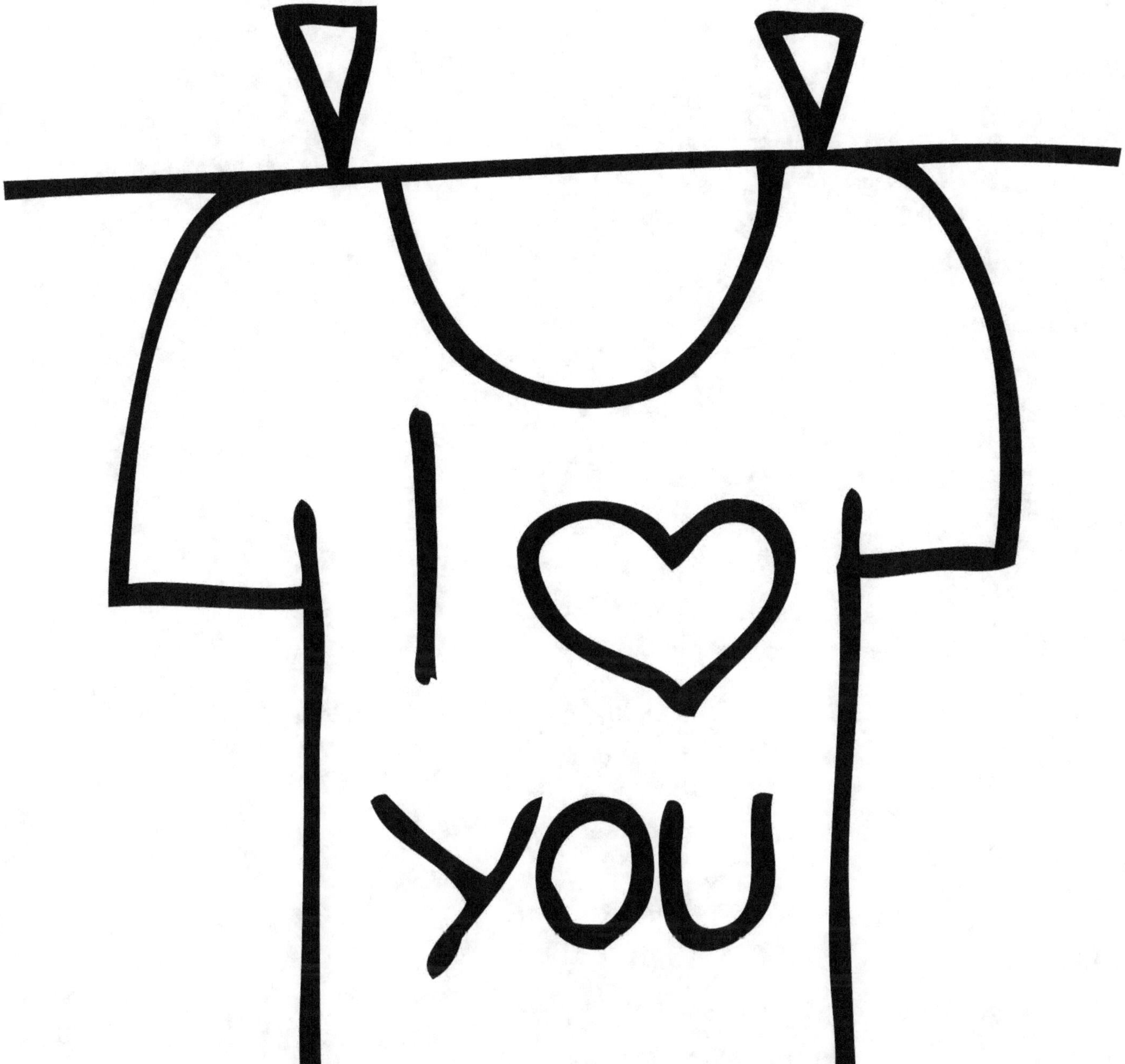
I ♡
YOU

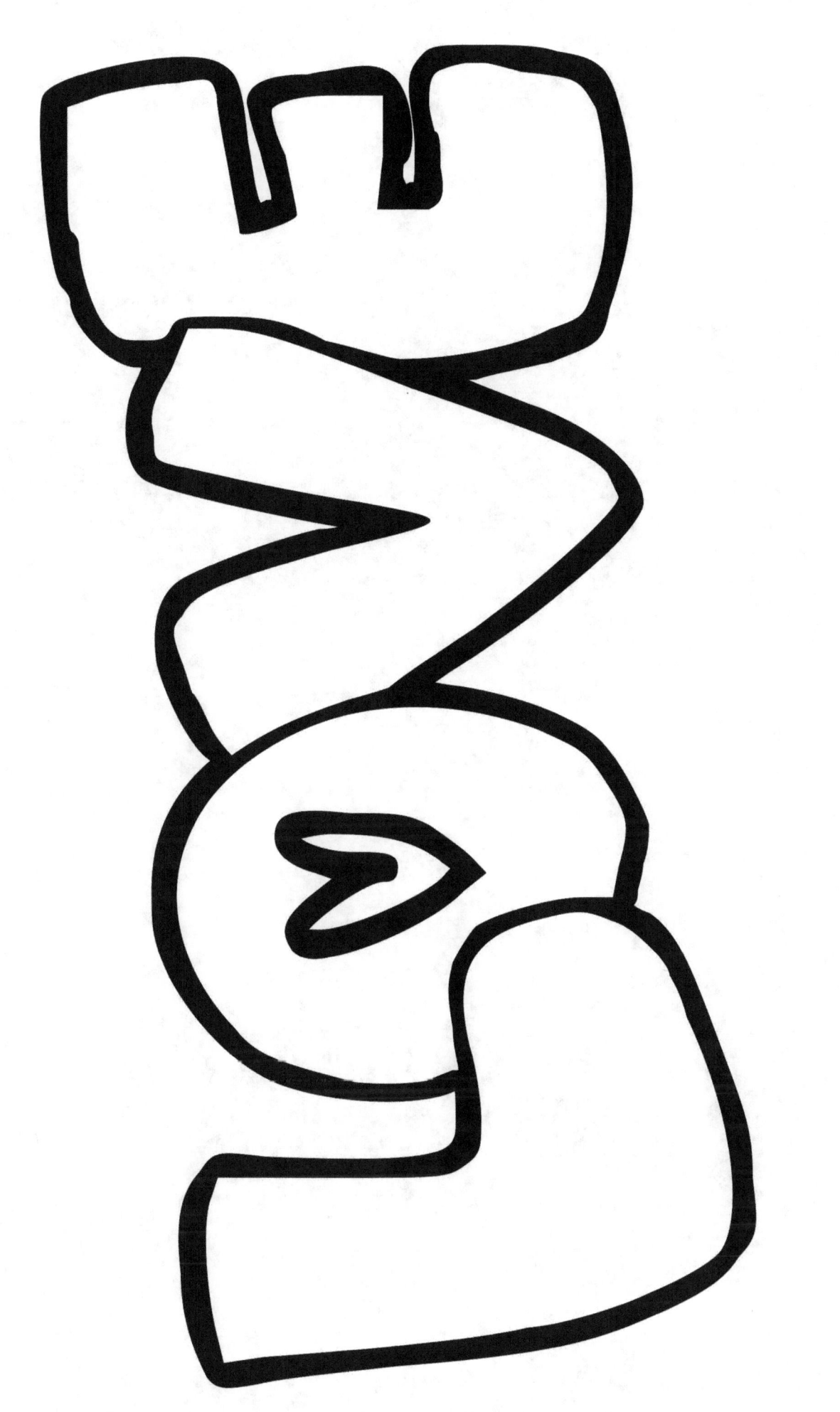

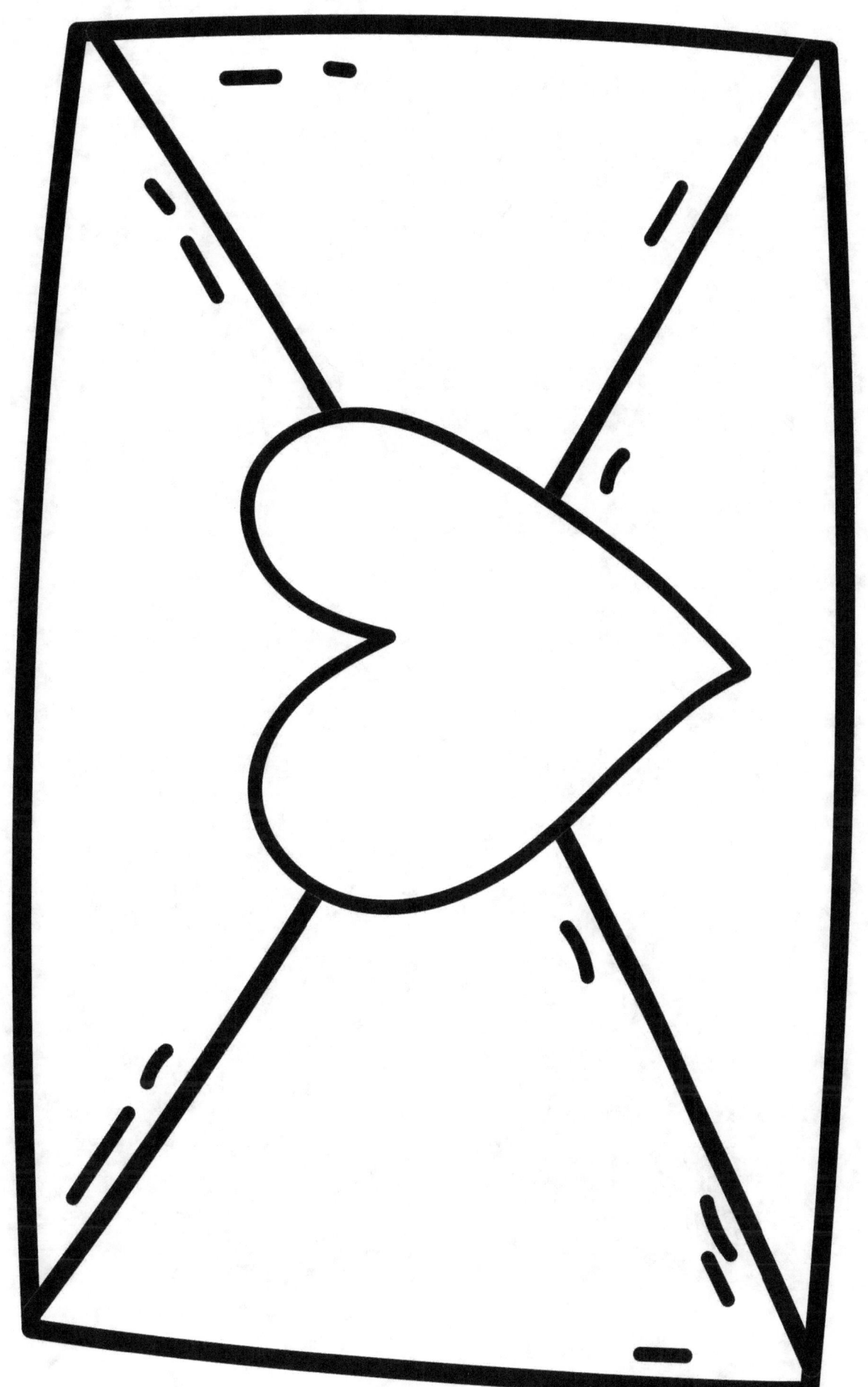

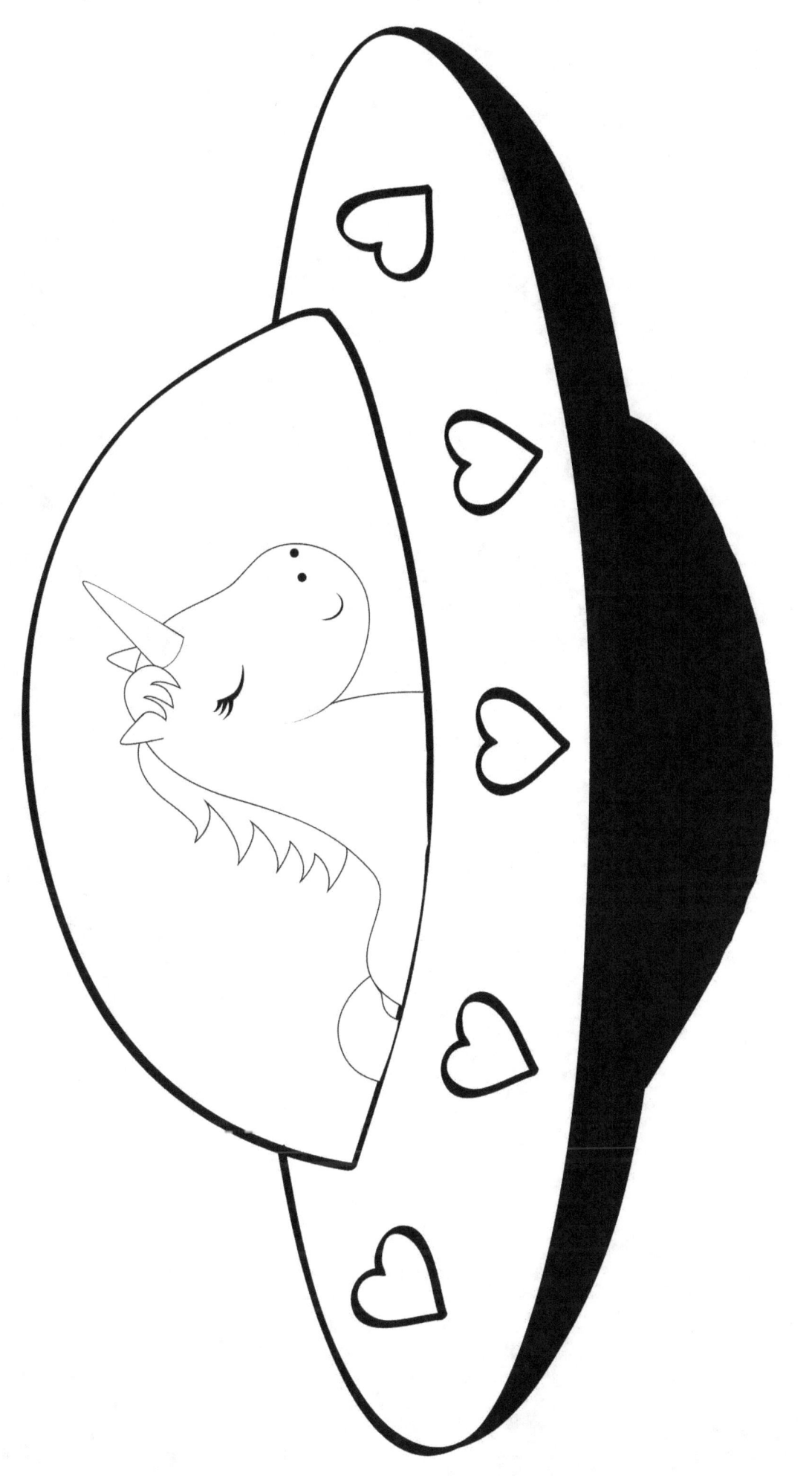

Kids' Activity Workbook Subscribe

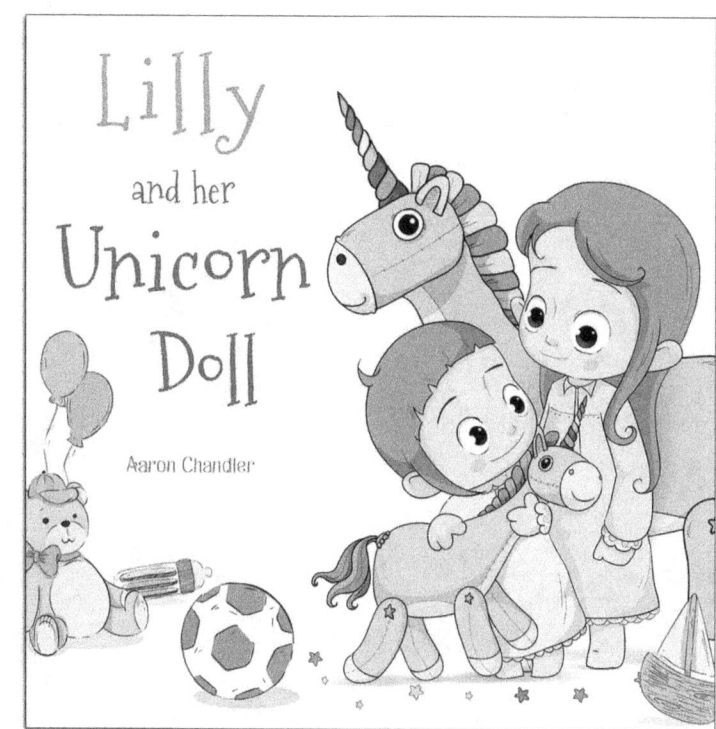

- Free 1st Book of Lilly and Unicorn Doll

- Book Update

- Promotion

- Kid Development Content

http://bit.ly/kid_kindle

www.ingramcontent.com/pod-product-compliance
Lightning Source LLC
Chambersburg PA
CBHW081603220526
45468CB00010B/2757